HOW TO ESCAPE THE MATRIX

By Harry Holland

Table of Contents

Chapter 1: Taking Action: Becoming the Chooser, Not the Chosen
Chapter 2: Escaping the 9-5 Myth: Embracing Remote Work and Being Your Own Boss
Chapter 3: Travel: Making the Most of Your Resources
Chapter 4: Building Passive Income Streams
Chapter 5: Breaking Free from News Consumption
Chapter 6: Balancing Online and Offline Life
Chapter 7: Minimalism: Living with Less
Chapter 8: Leading instead of Following: Trailblazing Your Path
Chapter 9: Overcoming External Limitations: Dealing with Family and Friends
Chapter 10: Embracing Life's Mystery: Finding Meaning in the Unknown
Chapter 11: Preparing for the Digital Nomad Lifestyle
Chapter 12: The Essence of the 4-Hour Work Week
Chapter 13: Pursuing Your Passion: Finding Work You Love
Chapter 14: The 80/20 Principle: Maximizing Productivity
Chapter 15: Automation and Delegation: Working Smarter, Not Harder
Chapter 16: Creating Effective To-Do and Not-to-Do Lists
Chapter 17: Evaluating Your Nomadic Lifestyle
Chapter 18: Building Self-Belief and Overcoming Doubts
Chapter 19: Following Your Passion: Taking Bold Action
Chapter 20: Making a Difference: Helping Others and Leaving a Legacy
Conclusion

CHAPTER 1: TAKING ACTION: BECOMING THE CHOOSER, NOT THE CHOSEN

In a world filled with limitless possibilities, it is all too easy to get lost in a sea of thoughts and ideas without taking any meaningful action. Many of us find ourselves trapped in a cycle of indecision, constantly analyzing and contemplating, but never actually moving forward. However, true liberation lies in breaking free from this stagnant state and becoming the chooser, rather than the chosen.

Taking action is the catalyst that propels us towards our goals and dreams. It is the fuel that ignites our potential and transforms mere thoughts into tangible realities. By actively engaging with the world around us, we gain control over our lives and open doors to endless opportunities. It is not enough to passively observe or wish for change; we must actively participate in creating the life we desire.

To develop a proactive mindset and embrace the power of taking action, we need to cultivate certain habits and perspectives. Let's explore some practical steps that can guide us on this transformative journey:

Define Your Vision: To become the chooser, you must first identify what it is that you truly want. Take the time to envision your ideal life, both personally and professionally. What are your passions, goals, and aspirations? Define them clearly and make them the guiding stars of your actions.

Set Clear Goals: Once you have a vision, break it down into actionable goals. Specific, measurable, attainable, relevant, and time-bound (SMART) goals provide a roadmap for your actions. Write them down and revisit them regularly to stay focused and motivated.

Overcome Analysis Paralysis: Often, the fear of making the wrong decision paralyzes us into inaction. Embrace the notion that there are no perfect choices and that mistakes are opportunities for growth. Trust your instincts, gather the necessary information, and make informed decisions without getting caught in an endless cycle of analysis.

Take Incremental Steps: Big dreams can be overwhelming, but remember that progress is achieved through small, consistent steps. Break down your goals into manageable tasks and take one step at a time. Celebrate each small victory, as they bring you closer to your ultimate vision.

Embrace Failure as Feedback: Failure is not the end; it is a stepping stone on the path to success. Learn from your mistakes, adapt, and persevere. Understand that setbacks are valuable lessons that guide you towards better choices and outcomes.

Cultivate a Bias for Action: Develop a mindset that values taking action over endless planning. Be willing to step out of your comfort zone and embrace the unknown. Start before you feel ready, for it is through action that you gain experience and confidence.

Practice Discipline and Consistency: Taking action requires discipline and consistency. Cultivate habits that support your goals and eliminate distractions that hinder your progress. Prioritize your time and energy on activities that align with your vision.

Seek Support and Accountability: Surround yourself with like-minded individuals who support and challenge you. Join communities or find mentors who can provide guidance and hold you accountable. Collaboration and support can fuel your motivation and keep you on track.

Embrace Adaptability: Life is ever-changing, and so are our goals and circumstances. Be adaptable and open to adjusting your course as needed. View challenges as opportunities for growth and learn to pivot when necessary.

Celebrate Progress: Recognize and celebrate your achievements along the way. Acknowledge the efforts you have put in and the milestones you have reached. Celebrating your progress reinforces positive behavior and boosts your motivation to continue taking action.

By implementing these practical steps and adopting a proactive mindset, you can break free from the inertia of inaction and become the driver of your own life. Remember, the power lies in your ability to take action and shape your reality. Embrace the role of the chooser, seize opportunities, and watch as your dreams transform into lived experiences.

Take a deep breath, step forward, and embark on this journey of self-discovery and empowerment. The choice is yours, and the time for action is now.

CHAPTER 2: ESCAPING THE 9-5 MYTH: EMBRACING REMOTE WORK AND BEING YOUR OWN BOSS

In today's interconnected world, the traditional 9-5 office job is no longer the only path to success and fulfillment. Remote work has emerged as a transformative opportunity, allowing individuals to break free from the constraints of traditional employment and embrace a lifestyle that offers freedom, flexibility, and the ability to be your own boss. In this chapter, we will explore the benefits of remote work and provide practical tips for finding remote work opportunities and establishing yourself as a freelancer or entrepreneur.

Embracing the Benefits of Remote Work

Freedom and Flexibility:
Remote work liberates you from the confines of a physical office space. You have the freedom to work from anywhere, whether it's a bustling cafe in a foreign city or the comfort of your own home. This flexibility allows you to design your work schedule around your personal preferences and optimize your productivity.

Increased Autonomy: As a remote worker, you have the opportunity to take ownership of your work and be your own boss. You have the autonomy to make decisions, set your own goals, and define your career trajectory. This level of independence can be incredibly empowering and fulfilling.

Work-Life Balance:
Remote work offers the potential for a healthier work-life balance. With the elimination of commuting and the ability to structure your day according to your needs, you can allocate time for personal pursuits, family, and self-care. This balance enhances overall well-being and satisfaction.

Finding Remote Work Opportunities:

Identify Your Skills: Start by identifying your skills and expertise. Consider what value you can offer to potential clients or employers in a remote work setting. Assess your strengths and passions to determine your niche and the type of remote work that aligns with your skills.

Freelancing Platforms: Explore freelancing platforms such as Upwork, Freelancer, or Fiverr. Create a compelling profile highlighting your skills and experience. Be proactive in searching for relevant projects and submitting proposals that demonstrate your capabilities.

Networking: Build a strong professional network in your desired field. Attend industry events, join online communities, and connect with like-minded professionals. Networking can lead to remote job opportunities through referrals and recommendations.

Remote Job Boards: Utilize remote job boards like Remote OK, We Work Remotely, or FlexJobs. These platforms specifically cater to remote work opportunities across various industries and provide a curated selection of remote job postings.

Direct Outreach: Research companies or organizations that embrace remote work and directly reach out to express your interest in remote positions. Craft personalized emails or LinkedIn messages highlighting your skills and how you can contribute to their remote team.

Establishing Yourself as a Freelancer or Entrepreneur:
Develop a Portfolio: Showcase your work and skills through a well-curated portfolio. Create a professional website or online portfolio that highlights your best projects, testimonials, and client feedback. This serves as a powerful tool for attracting potential clients or employers.

Build Your Personal Brand: Cultivate a strong personal brand that reflects your expertise and values. Use social media platforms like LinkedIn, Twitter, or Instagram to share valuable content, engage with industry professionals, and establish yourself as an authority in your field.

Nurture Client Relationships: Deliver exceptional work and provide excellent customer service to build long-term relationships with clients. Word-of-mouth referrals and positive testimonials are invaluable for attracting new clients and securing repeat business.

Continuous Learning: Stay updated with industry trends, tools, and best practices. Invest in your professional development by taking online courses, attending webinars, or joining relevant communities. Continuous learning enhances your skills and keeps you competitive in the remote work landscape.

Diversify Your Income Streams: Explore multiple income streams to ensure stability and resilience. Consider offering a mix of services, creating digital products, or developing passive income streams that align with your expertise. Diversification mitigates risk and provides greater financial security.

Embracing remote work and becoming your own boss requires courage, adaptability, and perseverance. By understanding the benefits of remote work, actively seeking opportunities, and establishing yourself as a freelancer or entrepreneur, you can break free from the 9-5 myth and create a fulfilling and prosperous career on your own terms. The possibilities are endless, and the world is your office. Take the leap and embrace the transformative power of remote work.

CHAPTER 3: TRAVEL: MAKING THE MOST OF YOUR RESOURCES

Travel is a fundamental aspect of the digital nomad lifestyle. It offers not only the opportunity to explore new places and cultures but also the chance to make the most of your resources, both financially and experientially. In this chapter, we will explore the financial advantages of living and working in lower-cost locations and provide practical examples of how to budget and manage your expenses while enjoying a nomadic lifestyle.

Financial Advantages of Lower-Cost Locations:

Cost of Living: One of the significant advantages of being a digital nomad is the ability to choose where you live. By selecting lower-cost locations, you can stretch your budget further and enjoy a higher quality of life. Countries or cities with a lower cost of living can offer affordable accommodation, transportation, food, and entertainment options.

Currency Exchange Rates: Understanding currency exchange rates can work in your favor as a digital nomad. Look for locations where your home currency is strong compared to the local currency. This can make everyday expenses more affordable and allow you to save money while living abroad.

Access to Affordable Healthcare: Some countries offer high-quality healthcare services at a fraction of the cost compared to other parts of the world. Research locations with reliable and affordable healthcare systems, ensuring that you have access to medical care while living as a digital nomad.

Tax Benefits: Depending on your country of origin and the tax laws in the locations you visit, you may be able to take advantage of tax benefits as a digital nomad. Explore the possibility of reducing your tax burden by legally establishing residency in a

tax-friendly jurisdiction.
Budgeting and Managing Expenses:

Research and Planning: Before embarking on your digital nomad journey, research the cost of living in your desired locations. Look into accommodation prices, transportation costs, food expenses, and other essentials. This research will help you create a realistic budget and determine how much you need to sustain your lifestyle.

Accommodation Options: Consider alternative accommodation options beyond traditional hotels. Renting apartments, staying in guesthouses, or using platforms like Airbnb can often be more cost-effective, especially for longer stays. Look for accommodations with basic amenities that meet your needs without breaking the bank.

Transportation: Optimize your transportation expenses by utilizing local public transportation systems, walking, or using affordable ride-sharing services. Research the most cost-effective ways to get around in each location and plan your transportation accordingly.

Dining: Eating out can quickly add up, so balance your expenses by cooking meals at home or opting for local street food. Explore local markets and grocery stores to buy fresh produce and ingredients. Not only will this help you save money, but it will also allow you to experience the local cuisine in a more authentic way.

Entertainment and Activities: Seek out low-cost or free activities and attractions in each location. Many cities offer free walking tours, public parks, museums with discounted or free entry days, and community events. Embrace the local culture and participate in activities that don't strain your budget.

Travel Insurance: Prioritize your health and well-being by investing in comprehensive travel insurance. While it adds to your expenses, it provides peace of mind and protects you from

unexpected medical costs or travel-related emergencies.
Embracing Resourceful Living:

Embrace Minimalism: Adopting a minimalist lifestyle can be especially beneficial as a digital nomad. Traveling light not only reduces your expenses but also allows for greater mobility and flexibility. Prioritize experiences over material possessions, and learn to appreciate the freedom that comes with owning less.

Work Exchange and Volunteering: Consider opportunities for work exchange or volunteering in exchange for accommodation or other benefits. Websites like Workaway, HelpX, and WWOOF connect travelers with hosts who offer free accommodation and meals in return for a few hours of work each day. This can be an excellent way to reduce expenses and immerse yourself in the local culture.

Coworking Spaces and Communities: Joining coworking spaces or digital nomad communities can provide access to a supportive network and shared resources. These spaces often offer affordable membership plans that include workspace, amenities, and networking opportunities. Engaging with fellow digital nomads can also lead to valuable insights and collaborations.

Local Networking and Collaboration: Build connections with locals and other digital nomads in the locations you visit. Attend meetups, networking events, and workshops relevant to your industry or interests. This not only expands your professional network but can also lead to collaborations, job opportunities, and shared resources.

Traveling as a digital nomad allows you to make the most of your resources, enabling you to experience diverse cultures, grow personally and professionally, and manage your expenses effectively. By leveraging the financial advantages of lower-cost locations, creating a budget, and embracing resourceful living, you can fully enjoy the nomadic lifestyle while maintaining financial stability. So pack your bags, explore the world, and savor the incredible opportunities that await you as a digital nomad.

CHAPTER 4: BUILDING PASSIVE INCOME STREAMS

Passive income is the key to financial independence and a vital component of the digital nomad lifestyle. It allows you to generate income while enjoying the freedom to travel, explore, and pursue your passions. In this chapter, we will discuss various ways to build passive income streams and offer practical advice on getting started and maintaining these sources of income.

Understanding Passive Income:

Definition: Passive income refers to earnings that are generated with minimal ongoing effort or time investment. It is income that continues to flow even when you're not actively working.
Importance for Digital Nomads: Passive income provides stability and financial security, freeing you from the constraints of traditional employment. It allows you to have more control over your time and focus on what truly matters to you.

Diversification: It's essential to diversify your passive income streams to minimize risk. Relying on a single source of passive income may be precarious, so explore multiple avenues to build a robust and sustainable income portfolio.

Generating Passive Income:

Writing a Book: Authoring a book can be a lucrative source of passive income. Choose a topic you're knowledgeable and passionate about, and self-publish your book through platforms like Amazon Kindle Direct Publishing (KDP). Invest time in marketing and promoting your book to reach a wider audience and maximize sales.

Creating Online Products: Develop digital products such as online courses, e-books, or software applications that provide value to a specific target audience. Once created, these products can be sold repeatedly without requiring significant additional effort.

Affiliate Marketing: Partner with companies and promote their products or services through affiliate marketing. Earn a commission for every sale or referral made through your unique affiliate links. Create valuable content and establish trust with your audience to maximize your affiliate marketing success.

Rental Properties: Investing in rental properties can be an excellent long-term strategy for generating passive income. Consider purchasing properties in desirable locations, manage them efficiently, and ensure a steady stream of rental income.

Dividend-Paying Stocks: Invest in dividend-paying stocks to earn regular income from your investments. Research and choose companies with a track record of consistent dividend payments and potential for long-term growth.

Peer-to-Peer Lending: Explore peer-to-peer lending platforms where you can lend money to individuals or businesses and earn interest on your investment. Conduct thorough due diligence and understand the risks associated with peer-to-peer lending before committing funds.

Digital Products or Services: Leverage your skills and expertise to create and sell digital products or offer digital services. Examples include graphic design, web development, content writing, consulting, or coaching. Build a strong online presence and market your services to attract clients.
Getting Started and Maintaining Passive Income Streams:

Research and Education: Before diving into any passive income venture, invest time in thorough research and education. Understand the potential risks, rewards, and requirements associated with each income stream.

Start Small: Begin with a single passive income stream and gradually expand your portfolio. Starting small allows you to gain experience, learn from any challenges, and refine your strategies before scaling up.

Consistency and Persistence: Building passive income takes time and effort. Be consistent in your efforts, and don't get discouraged by initial slow progress. Persistence is key to long-term success.

Automation and Systems: Implement automation and systems to streamline your passive income streams. Leverage technology and tools to automate processes, such as payment collection, content distribution, or customer support.

Monitor and Adjust: Regularly assess the performance of your passive income sources and make necessary adjustments. Stay updated with market trends, consumer preferences, and industry changes to ensure your income streams remain relevant and profitable.

Adaptability and Innovation: Continuously explore new opportunities and adapt to evolving market dynamics. Embrace innovation and stay open to trying new strategies or exploring emerging industries that align with your skills and interests.

Building passive income streams is a journey that requires dedication, persistence, and continuous learning. By diversifying your income sources, investing time and effort in creating valuable products or services, and staying adaptable, you can enjoy the freedom and financial stability that passive income brings. Take control of your financial future, embark on this exciting path, and unlock the true potential of the digital nomad lifestyle.

CHAPTER 5: BREAKING FREE FROM NEWS CONSUMPTION

In today's fast-paced digital world, news consumption has become a ubiquitous part of our daily lives. We find ourselves constantly bombarded with information, headlines, and updates, often without realizing the impact it has on our well-being and personal growth. In this chapter, we will explore the negative effects of excessive news consumption and provide practical strategies for reducing news intake and focusing on positive and constructive information.

The Negative Effects of Excessive News Consumption:

Information Overload: The constant influx of news can lead to information overload, making it challenging to discern what is truly important and relevant.
Anxiety and Stress: Consuming news, particularly negative and sensationalized stories, can increase anxiety levels and contribute to feelings of stress and overwhelm.
Loss of Focus: Excessive news consumption can distract us from our goals and priorities, diverting our attention away from personal growth and productivity.
Biased Perspectives: News sources often have their own agendas, and consuming news from a single source can result in biased perspectives and limited understanding of complex issues.
Emotional Impact: News stories can elicit strong emotional reactions, affecting our mood, mindset, and overall well-being.
Assessing Your News Consumption Habits:

Awareness: Reflect on your news consumption habits and evaluate how much time and energy you spend on consuming news.
Sources: Consider the reliability and credibility of the news sources you follow. Are they balanced, unbiased, and reputable?

Emotional Response: Take note of your emotional reactions to news stories. Do they uplift or drain your energy? Are they contributing positively to your mindset and personal growth?
Strategies for Reducing News Intake:

Set Boundaries: Establish specific times during the day for consuming news, and limit the duration. Avoid checking news first thing in the morning or before bed, as it can disrupt your peace of mind.

Select Trusted Sources: Choose a few reliable news sources that provide balanced and fact-checked information. Avoid sensationalized or clickbait headlines that prioritize generating attention over providing accurate news.

Create a News-Free Zone: Designate certain areas or times in your day where you consciously avoid consuming news. This can be during meals, breaks, or when engaging in activities that require focus and presence.

Curate Your News Feed: Customize your social media and news app settings to filter out unnecessary news content and prioritize positive and constructive information. Unfollow or mute accounts that consistently share negative or anxiety-inducing news.

Seek Diverse Perspectives: Expand your horizons by seeking news from diverse sources and perspectives. This helps you develop a more comprehensive understanding of complex issues and reduces the risk of falling into an echo chamber.

Engage in Meaningful Conversations: Instead of endlessly consuming news, allocate time to engage in thoughtful discussions with others. This allows you to gain insights, exchange ideas, and broaden your understanding of various topics.

Focus on Solutions: Instead of dwelling on problems highlighted in the news, shift your attention towards constructive and actionable solutions. Seek out news stories that inspire positive change and showcase individuals or organizations making a difference.

Cultivating a Positive Information Diet:

Seek Inspiration: Consume content that uplifts and inspires you. This can include personal development books, podcasts, or documentaries that promote growth, motivation, and well-being.
Invest in Learning: Allocate time for learning and acquiring new skills. Engage in online courses, workshops, or educational platforms that align with your interests and goals.
Balance News with Other Topics: Expand your knowledge beyond news by exploring diverse subjects such as literature, arts, science, philosophy, or history. This broadens your perspective and fosters intellectual curiosity.
Practice Mindfulness: Engage in mindfulness techniques such as meditation, deep breathing, or journaling to cultivate present-moment awareness and reduce the influence of external distractions, including news.

By consciously reducing news consumption and curating a positive information diet, you can reclaim your time, energy, and focus for personal growth, meaningful connections, and pursuing your passions. Remember, the quality of information you consume greatly influences your mindset, well-being, and ability to thrive in the digital nomad lifestyle. Choose wisely and break free from the confines of excessive news consumption to embrace a more fulfilling and intentional life.

CHAPTER 6: BALANCING ONLINE AND OFFLINE LIFE

In our increasingly connected world, it's easy to get caught up in the allure of the digital realm. The internet offers us endless opportunities for communication, work, and entertainment, but it's crucial not to lose sight of the importance of real-world connections and experiences. In this chapter, we will highlight the significance of maintaining a healthy balance between our online and offline lives and provide practical ways to limit social media usage while prioritizing face-to-face interactions.

The Importance of Real-World Connections:

Human Connection: While technology allows us to connect with people from all over the world, nothing can replace the depth and richness of face-to-face interactions. Real-world connections foster empathy, understanding, and a sense of belonging.

Personal Growth: Engaging in meaningful conversations and shared experiences with others can broaden our perspectives, challenge our assumptions, and contribute to personal growth and self-discovery.

Well-Being: Spending quality time with loved ones and building relationships offline promotes emotional well-being, reduces feelings of loneliness, and enhances overall life satisfaction.

Practical Ways to Limit Social Media Usage:

Set Boundaries: Establish specific time blocks during the day dedicated to social media use. Define clear start and end times to prevent mindless scrolling and ensure you allocate time for other activities.

Disable Notifications: Minimize distractions by turning off notifications from social media apps. This reduces the temptation to constantly check your phone and allows you to be more present in your offline experiences.

Create Device-Free Zones: Designate certain areas or times where you avoid using electronic devices altogether. This can be during meals, social gatherings, or before bedtime to promote better sleep quality.

Practice Digital Detox: Take periodic breaks from social media by abstaining from it for a day, a weekend, or even longer periods. Use this time to engage in hobbies, connect with nature, or focus on personal pursuits.

Unfollow and Curate: Review your social media feeds and unfollow accounts that do not add value to your life or negatively impact your well-being. Curate your feeds to prioritize content that aligns with your interests and values.

Find Alternative Activities: Replace social media browsing with activities that bring you joy and fulfillment. Explore hobbies, read books, engage in physical exercise, or spend quality time with friends and family.

Prioritizing Face-to-Face Interactions:

Quality Time: Make a conscious effort to spend quality time with loved ones and friends in person. Plan outings, meet for meals, or engage in shared activities that foster genuine connections and create lasting memories.

Join Local Communities: Seek out local communities, clubs, or interest groups that align with your hobbies and passions. Participating in group activities allows you to meet like-minded individuals and build meaningful relationships.

Networking Events: Attend networking events, conferences, or industry meetups related to your professional interests. These events provide opportunities to connect with professionals, exchange ideas, and build valuable connections.

Volunteer or Join Causes: Get involved in volunteer work or community initiatives that resonate with you. Engaging in activities that serve others allows you to connect with people who share your values and make a positive impact together.

Travel and Cultural Immersion: While traveling, make an effort to immerse yourself in local cultures, interact with locals, and participate in cultural events or activities. This provides unique opportunities for cross-cultural understanding and meaningful connections.

Practicing Digital Balance:

Mindful Technology Use: Be mindful of how you use technology and the purpose behind your online activities. Avoid mindless scrolling and instead engage in intentional and purposeful online interactions.

Set Priorities: Determine your priorities and allocate time accordingly. Create a schedule that allows for a healthy balance between work, online activities, and offline experiences.

Establish Offline Rituals: Cultivate offline rituals that bring you joy and allow you to disconnect from the digital world. This could be practicing a hobby, engaging in physical activities, or spending time in nature.

Practice Presence: When engaging in face-to-face interactions, practice being fully present. Put away your phone, actively listen, and engage in meaningful conversations. Show genuine interest in the people around you.

Reflect and Evaluate: Regularly reflect on your online and offline experiences. Assess whether you feel fulfilled and balanced in your interactions. Make adjustments as needed to ensure your digital and real-world lives are in harmony.

By consciously striving for a balance between our online and offline lives, we can cultivate deeper connections, experience personal growth, and find greater fulfillment in the digital nomad lifestyle. Remember, technology is a tool that should enhance our lives, not dominate them. Find the balance that works best for you, and embrace the richness of both the digital and real-world experiences available to you.

CHAPTER 7: MINIMALISM: LIVING WITH LESS

In a world driven by consumerism and the pursuit of material possessions, embracing minimalism can be a powerful antidote. Minimalism is not just about owning fewer things; it's a mindset that encourages intentional living, focusing on what truly matters, and finding happiness in non-materialistic pursuits. In this chapter, we will explore the benefits of living a simple and minimalist lifestyle and provide practical tips for decluttering, organizing, and finding fulfillment with less.

The Benefits of Minimalism:

Clarity and Focus: By eliminating excess belongings, you create a physical and mental space that allows you to focus on what truly matters in your life. Minimalism helps clarify your values, priorities, and goals.
Reduced Stress and Overwhelm: The constant accumulation of possessions can lead to clutter, which contributes to stress and a feeling of being overwhelmed. Minimalism promotes a clutter-free environment, leading to a calmer and more peaceful mindset.
Financial Freedom: Minimalism encourages mindful consumption and helps you break free from the cycle of endless material acquisition. By spending less on unnecessary items, you can save money, reduce debt, and achieve financial independence.
Environmental Sustainability: Consumerism has a significant impact on the environment. By adopting a minimalist lifestyle, you reduce your carbon footprint, minimize waste, and contribute to a more sustainable future.
Decluttering and Organizing:

Start Small: Begin decluttering by focusing on one area at a time. Start with a drawer, a shelf, or a small room. Breaking the process into smaller tasks makes it more manageable and less overwhelming.

The Minimalist Mindset: When decluttering, ask yourself if an item adds value to your life. If it doesn't serve a purpose or bring you joy, consider letting it go. Embrace the mindset of keeping only what truly matters.

The Four-Box Method: Use the four-box method when sorting through your belongings. Label four boxes as "Keep," "Donate/Sell," "Trash," and "Undecided." Place each item in the appropriate box based on its value and usefulness to you.

One-In, One-Out Rule: Implement the one-in, one-out rule for new purchases. For every new item you bring into your life, let go of something else. This practice helps maintain a clutter-free environment and encourages mindful consumption.

Organizational Systems: Once you've decluttered, establish efficient organizational systems. Use storage containers, labels, and designated spaces for different items. Keep frequently used items easily accessible and maintain a habit of returning things to their designated places.

Finding Happiness in Non-Materialistic Pursuits:

Experiences over Possessions: Shift your focus from acquiring material possessions to investing in experiences. Allocate your resources toward activities that create lasting memories, such as travel, learning new skills, or spending quality time with loved ones.

Cultivate Gratitude: Practice gratitude for what you have rather than constantly yearning for more. Reflect on the things that bring you joy and appreciate the simple pleasures in life.

Define Your Values: Clarify your values and align your actions with them. Determine what truly matters to you and prioritize activities and relationships that support those values.

Mindful Consumption: Before making a purchase, evaluate whether it aligns with your values and brings genuine value to your life. Avoid impulsive buying and consider the long-term impact of your choices.

Emotional Detachment: Let go of attachments to material

possessions and recognize that true happiness doesn't come from external things. Embrace the freedom that comes with detaching your self-worth from what you own.

Extending Minimalism to Digital Spaces:

Digital Decluttering: Apply minimalist principles to your digital life as well. Clean up your email inbox, organize your digital files, and delete unused apps and software.
Digital Detox: Take regular breaks from digital devices and platforms. Establish screen-free periods during the day, create technology-free zones in your home, and engage in offline activities that nourish your mind and body.
Mindful Digital Consumption: Be intentional about your online activities. Consume content mindfully, focusing on quality over quantity. Unfollow accounts or unsubscribe from newsletters that no longer serve you positively.
Digital Minimalism Apps: Utilize digital tools and apps that help you track and limit your time spent on social media and other digital distractions. Set boundaries and create healthier digital habits.

By embracing minimalism, you can simplify your life, free yourself from the burden of excess possessions, and discover a greater sense of fulfillment. Remember that minimalism is a personal journey, and there is no one-size-fits-all approach. Find what works best for you, align your lifestyle with your values, and enjoy the freedom and peace that come with living with less.

CHAPTER 8: LEADING INSTEAD OF FOLLOWING: TRAILBLAZING YOUR PATH

In a world that often encourages conformity and following the crowd, there is immense power in becoming a leader and forging your own path. This chapter will explore the advantages of embracing leadership in both personal and professional life, providing practical examples of how you can take initiative and become a trailblazer. By stepping into a leadership role, you can shape your own destiny and create a life that aligns with your values and aspirations.

Embracing Personal Leadership:

Define Your Vision: Take time to reflect on your values, passions, and long-term goals. Clarify what you want to achieve in your personal life and envision the path that will lead you there. Having a clear vision empowers you to make decisions and take action aligned with your aspirations.

Cultivate Self-Awareness: Understand your strengths, weaknesses, and areas for growth. Self-awareness allows you to leverage your strengths effectively and develop strategies to overcome challenges. Seek feedback from others and continually strive for personal development.

Take Ownership of Your Life: Recognize that you are responsible for your own happiness and success. Instead of waiting for opportunities to come to you, actively seek them out. Be proactive in setting goals, making decisions, and taking steps towards the life you desire.

Embrace Risk and Failure: Leaders understand that taking risks and experiencing failure are essential parts of the journey. Embrace discomfort, learn from your failures, and see them as valuable lessons that contribute to your growth and resilience.

Leading in Professional Life:

Identify Your Unique Value: Determine what sets you apart from others in your professional field. Identify your unique skills, experiences, and perspectives that can bring value to organizations or clients. Emphasize and leverage these strengths to position yourself as a leader in your industry.

Continual Learning and Skill Development: Commit to lifelong learning and stay updated with industry trends and advancements. Seek out opportunities for professional development, whether through courses, workshops, or networking events. By continuously improving your skills, you position yourself as a leader who can adapt to changing environments.

Take Initiative: Instead of waiting for instructions or permission, take proactive steps to create opportunities for yourself. Identify problems or areas for improvement within your work environment and take the initiative to propose solutions or implement positive changes. By demonstrating leadership qualities, you become invaluable to your team or clients.

Build a Network: Surround yourself with like-minded individuals who share your drive and ambition. Attend industry events, join professional associations, and actively engage in networking opportunities. Cultivate relationships with mentors who can guide and support your growth as a leader.

Leading with Integrity and Empathy:

Lead by Example: Demonstrate integrity and ethical behavior in all your actions. Your integrity will inspire trust and respect from others, enhancing your influence as a leader. Be a role model for professionalism, honesty, and transparency.

Practice Empathetic Communication: Develop strong interpersonal skills and practice empathetic communication. Seek to understand the perspectives and needs of others, and communicate with empathy and respect. Effective leaders listen actively and foster a collaborative and inclusive work environment.

Delegate and Empower Others: As a leader, delegate tasks and responsibilities to others, providing them with opportunities to grow and develop their own skills. Empower your team members by trusting their abilities and supporting their professional growth. By creating a supportive and empowering work environment, you cultivate a culture of leadership within your team.

Trailblazing Your Path:

Embrace Creativity and Innovation: Challenge the status quo and embrace a mindset of innovation. Seek out new ideas, approaches, and solutions to problems. Encourage creativity within yourself and those around you, fostering a culture that values innovation.

Embrace Diversity and Inclusion: Recognize the value of diverse perspectives and experiences. Foster an inclusive work environment where all individuals feel valued and heard. Embracing diversity enhances creativity, problem-solving, and overall team performance.

Embrace Continuous Improvement: Strive for excellence in all that you do. Continually evaluate your performance and seek feedback to identify areas for improvement. Embrace a growth mindset that allows you to learn from setbacks and continuously evolve as a leader.

By embracing leadership and trailblazing your path, you seize control of your personal and professional journey. Through personal leadership, you define your vision and take ownership of your life. In professional life, you position yourself as a leader who brings unique value, leads with integrity and empathy, and fosters innovation and inclusivity. Remember, leadership is not limited to titles or positions—it is a mindset and a choice to step forward, take action, and create a meaningful impact on the world around you.

CHAPTER 9: OVERCOMING EXTERNAL LIMITATIONS: DEALING WITH FAMILY AND FRIENDS

Breaking free from societal expectations and well-meaning but limiting influences can be one of the most challenging aspects of pursuing a non-traditional lifestyle like digital nomadism. The support and understanding of family and friends play a significant role in your journey towards freedom and fulfillment. In this chapter, we will address the challenges you may face in overcoming external limitations and offer practical advice on how to communicate with loved ones and gain their support for your chosen path.

Reflect on Your Motivations:

Before engaging in conversations with family and friends, take the time to reflect on your motivations for pursuing a digital nomad lifestyle. Clarify your values, aspirations, and the personal growth opportunities you envision. Understanding your own reasons will enable you to communicate your desires more effectively and authentically.

Open and Honest Communication:

Approach conversations with loved ones in an open and non-confrontational manner. Choose an appropriate time and place where everyone feels comfortable. Be honest about your dreams, aspirations, and the lifestyle you wish to create. Explain the benefits and opportunities that come with being a digital nomad, such as personal freedom, cultural experiences, and career growth.

Educate and Inform:

Many family members and friends may not fully understand the concept of digital nomadism or the opportunities it presents. Take the time to educate them on the growing trend of remote work and the benefits it offers. Share success stories of digital nomads who have built fulfilling lives and careers on their own terms. Provide resources, articles, or books that can help them better understand your chosen path.

Address Concerns and Misconceptions:

Family and friends may express concerns about your financial stability, job security, or well-being. Listen empathetically to their concerns and address them with well-thought-out responses. Assure them that you have considered these aspects and have plans in place to mitigate risks. Share examples of successful digital nomads who have achieved financial stability and personal growth.

Seek Supportive Allies:

Identify family members or friends who are open-minded and supportive. Share your dreams and aspirations with them first, as they are more likely to understand and support your choices. Having a strong support network will provide encouragement and understanding during challenging times.

Demonstrate Success and Commitment:

Actions speak louder than words. Show your loved ones that you are committed to making your digital nomad lifestyle a success. Take steps towards building a sustainable career, saving money, and consistently working on personal growth. When they see your dedication and positive results, it can help alleviate their concerns and gain their support.

Set Boundaries:

It is crucial to establish clear boundaries with family and friends. Make it known what kind of support you need and what topics are off-limits for discussion. Communicate your need for respect and understanding regarding your chosen lifestyle. By setting boundaries, you create an environment that fosters mutual respect and reduces potential conflicts.

Be Patient and Understanding:

Change can be challenging for both you and your loved ones. Understand that they may need time to adjust to your new lifestyle and mindset. Be patient and empathetic as they process their own emotions and concerns. Show understanding and respect for their perspectives, even if they don't fully align with yours.

Seek Like-Minded Communities:

Connect with other digital nomads and like-minded individuals who understand and support your choices. Online communities, forums, and social media groups can provide a sense of belonging and valuable advice. Surrounding yourself with people who share similar aspirations can help you feel supported and understood.

Remember, gaining the support of your family and friends may not happen overnight. It requires ongoing communication, understanding, and patience. Be true to yourself, stay committed to your goals, and continue to demonstrate the positive impact your chosen lifestyle has on your life and well-being. As you navigate external limitations, know that you are not alone, and many others have successfully overcome similar challenges on their journey to living life on their own terms.

CHAPTER 10: EMBRACING LIFE'S MYSTERY: FINDING MEANING IN THE UNKNOWN

Life is a journey filled with mystery, and embracing the unknown can lead to profound personal growth and fulfillment. In this chapter, we will explore the existential aspect of life and delve into the beauty of embracing life's mysteries. By doing so, we can find meaning in our experiences and discover joy in the journey.

Embrace Curiosity:

Cultivate a mindset of curiosity and wonder. Approach each day with an open heart and an eagerness to explore the unknown. Curiosity fuels personal growth, expands your perspective, and allows you to make meaningful connections with the world around you. Ask questions, seek new experiences, and be open to unexpected discoveries.

Practice Mindfulness:

Engage in mindfulness practices to anchor yourself in the present moment. Mindfulness helps you appreciate the beauty of each experience, even in the midst of uncertainty. By focusing on the here and now, you can fully immerse yourself in the mysteries unfolding before you.

Embrace Change:

Life is ever-changing, and embracing change is essential to finding meaning in the unknown. Instead of resisting change, view it as an opportunity for growth and transformation. Embrace the uncertainty that comes with change and trust that it will lead you to new and exciting paths.

Embrace Uncertainty:
Uncertainty can be uncomfortable, but it is also a gateway to growth and possibility. Rather than fearing the unknown,

embrace it with courage and resilience. Accept that life's mysteries cannot always be explained or controlled, and find solace in the beauty of uncertainty.

Find Beauty in Imperfection:

Perfection is an illusion that can hinder our ability to embrace the unknown. Instead, find beauty in imperfection. Recognize that life's mysteries often lie in the unexpected twists and turns, the flaws, and the moments of vulnerability. Embrace the imperfect nature of life and find meaning in its nuances.

Embrace Serendipity:

Serendipitous moments are magical occurrences that can lead to remarkable experiences and connections. Stay open to serendipity by being present, following your intuition, and saying yes to unexpected opportunities. Embracing serendipity allows you to fully immerse yourself in the mysteries that life presents.

Embrace Personal Growth:

Personal growth is intimately connected to embracing life's mysteries. It is through challenges, uncertainties, and stepping outside of our comfort zones that we grow the most. Embrace personal growth as an integral part of your journey, and see it as an opportunity to uncover hidden truths and find deeper meaning.

Connect with Others:

Meaningful connections with others can provide insight, support, and new perspectives on life's mysteries. Engage in deep conversations, seek out diverse relationships, and foster a sense of community. Through these connections, you can share experiences, learn from others, and collectively navigate the mysteries of life.

Engage in Self-Reflection:

Take time for self-reflection to explore your own beliefs, values, and desires. Self-reflection allows you to gain clarity and understanding of yourself, helping you navigate life's mysteries with intention and purpose. Engage in practices such as journaling, meditation, or contemplative walks to deepen your self-awareness.

Embrace the Journey:

Remember that life is not solely about reaching a destination; it is about the journey itself. Embrace the ups and downs, the twists and turns, and the unknown pathways that lie ahead. Find joy in the process of exploration, growth, and self-discovery, knowing that the journey itself is where true meaning resides.

By embracing life's mysteries, we open ourselves up to a world of possibilities, growth, and fulfillment. Embrace the unknown with curiosity, mindfulness, and a willingness to let go of control. Find beauty in imperfection, connect with others, and engage in self-reflection. As you navigate the mysteries of life, remember that it is in the journey that you will find true meaning and a life lived on your own terms.

CHAPTER 11: PREPARING FOR THE DIGITAL NOMAD LIFESTYLE

Embarking on the digital nomad lifestyle is an exciting and transformative journey. However, it requires careful preparation and planning to ensure a smooth transition. In this chapter, we will provide practical advice on how to prepare financially, emotionally, and logistically for this nomadic lifestyle. Additionally, we will discuss potential challenges that may arise and provide strategies for overcoming them.

Financial Preparation:

Assess Your Current Financial Situation:
Take the time to evaluate your current financial health. Understand your income, expenses, and savings. Assess any outstanding debts or financial obligations you have. This evaluation will give you a clear understanding of your financial standing and help you determine how long you can sustain yourself during the transition.

Create a Realistic Budget:
Design a budget that aligns with your desired digital nomad lifestyle. Consider factors such as accommodation costs, transportation, meals, and other living expenses specific to the locations you plan to visit. Be diligent in tracking your spending and find ways to optimize your budget to ensure financial stability.

Save an Emergency Fund:
Building an emergency fund is essential for any lifestyle change. Aim to save at least three to six months' worth of living expenses. This fund will serve as a safety net in case of unexpected expenses or temporary disruptions in income while you adjust to the digital nomad lifestyle.

Explore Income Streams:
Diversify your sources of income to ensure financial stability. Consider remote job opportunities, freelance work, or creating online products that generate passive income. Having multiple income streams will provide flexibility and mitigate potential income fluctuations.

Emotional Preparation:

Manage Expectations:
Recognize that the digital nomad lifestyle is not without its challenges. It is important to manage your expectations and be prepared for the realities of living and working in different environments. Embrace the uncertainty and be open to adapting to new situations and cultures.

Cultivate Resilience:
Building emotional resilience will help you navigate the ups and downs of the digital nomad lifestyle. Practice self-care, engage in mindfulness techniques, and develop strategies to manage stress effectively. Surround yourself with a supportive community of fellow digital nomads who understand the unique challenges you may face.

Develop Flexibility:
Flexibility is key when embracing the digital nomad lifestyle. Be adaptable to changes in your plans and environments. Cultivate a mindset that embraces new experiences and challenges. This flexibility will enable you to make the most of your journey and navigate any unexpected circumstances.

Logistical Preparation:

Secure Reliable Internet Access:
As a digital nomad, having a stable internet connection is vital. Research and identify reliable internet options in the locations you plan to visit. Consider backup plans, such as mobile hotspots or coworking spaces, to ensure uninterrupted connectivity.

Plan Accommodations and Transportation:
Research and book accommodations in advance, especially during peak travel seasons. Consider long-term rentals or house-sitting opportunities to minimize costs. Additionally, research transportation options within your chosen destinations to optimize travel expenses and maximize convenience.

Streamline Your Belongings:
Minimize the belongings you carry with you to maintain mobility and reduce unnecessary weight. Prioritize essential items, such as clothing, electronics, and work-related tools. Embrace a minimalist approach and consider storage options for items you don't need during your nomadic journey.

Maintain Legal Compliance:
Ensure you have the necessary visas and permits for the countries you plan to visit. Research and understand the legal requirements for working remotely and the tax implications associated with your chosen lifestyle. Seek professional advice if needed to ensure compliance with local regulations.

Preparing for Challenges:

Loneliness and Social Connection:
The digital nomad lifestyle can sometimes lead to feelings of loneliness and isolation. Prioritize building social connections by participating in local communities, attending coworking events, or joining digital nomad forums. Seek out like-minded individuals who can offer support and companionship.

Work-Life Balance:
Maintaining a healthy work-life balance is crucial as a digital nomad. Set clear boundaries between work and leisure time. Establish a dedicated workspace and define specific working hours. Prioritize self-care activities and make time for exploring the local culture and attractions.

Health and Safety:

Prioritize your health and safety while traveling. Research and invest in travel insurance that covers medical emergencies and unexpected events. Stay informed about local health risks and ensure you have access to necessary vaccinations and medications.

Time Management and Productivity:
Establish effective time management strategies to stay productive and focused. Set goals, prioritize tasks, and eliminate distractions. Experiment with productivity techniques such as the Pomodoro Technique or time blocking to optimize your work efficiency.

In summary, preparing for the digital nomad lifestyle requires thorough financial planning, emotional resilience, and logistical organization. Assess your finances, cultivate flexibility, and prepare for potential challenges. By taking proactive steps and adopting a proactive mindset, you will be well-equipped to embrace the nomadic lifestyle and embark on an exciting journey of freedom and self-discovery.

CHAPTER 12: THE ESSENCE OF THE 4-HOUR WORK WEEK

In this chapter, we will explore the essence of Tim Ferriss' renowned book, "The 4-Hour Work Week," and how its key principles can be applied to the digital nomad lifestyle. By understanding and implementing the strategies shared in this book, you can optimize your time management, increase productivity, and achieve a better work-life balance. Let's dive into the practical examples of time management and productivity strategies that can transform your digital nomad journey.

Define Your Goals and Priorities:
Begin by identifying your long-term goals and priorities. What do you truly want to achieve as a digital nomad? By having a clear vision, you can align your actions with your aspirations. Create a list of your top priorities and use it as a guiding compass for decision-making.

Apply the Pareto Principle:
The Pareto Principle, also known as the 80/20 rule, suggests that 20% of your efforts result in 80% of your desired outcomes. Identify the tasks and activities that contribute most significantly to your goals. Focus your energy on those high-impact tasks, delegating or eliminating less productive activities. This principle allows you to work smarter, not harder.

Eliminate Time-Wasting Activities:
Audit your daily routines and identify time-wasting activities that do not contribute to your goals. This could include excessive time spent on social media, indulging in unproductive conversations, or engaging in low-value tasks. Minimize or eliminate these distractions to regain control of your time.

Practice Parkinson's Law:

Parkinson's Law states that work expands to fill the time available for its completion. Apply this principle to your advantage by setting strict deadlines for tasks. By imposing time constraints, you increase focus and productivity. Break tasks into smaller, manageable chunks and allocate specific time blocks for their completion.

Embrace Outsourcing and Delegation:
As a digital nomad, you have the opportunity to leverage outsourcing and delegation to lighten your workload. Identify tasks that can be effectively handled by others, such as virtual assistants or freelancers, and delegate accordingly. This frees up your time to focus on higher-value activities that align with your core competencies.

Automate Routine Processes:
Automation is a powerful tool for digital nomads. Identify repetitive tasks or processes that can be automated to save time and effort. This could include email filters and autoresponders, social media scheduling tools, or automated invoicing and payment systems. Leverage technology to streamline your workflow and increase efficiency.

Optimize Communication Channels:
Effective communication is essential for remote work. Evaluate the communication channels you use and optimize them for efficiency. Choose platforms that facilitate clear and concise communication, such as project management tools, video conferencing software, or collaboration platforms. Streamlining communication reduces time spent on unnecessary back-and-forth and ensures effective collaboration with team members or clients.

Embrace Work-Life Integration:
Rather than striving for a strict separation of work and personal life, aim for work-life integration. Design your schedule in a way that allows you to pursue your passions and enjoy personal

experiences while also meeting work commitments. Embrace the flexibility that the digital nomad lifestyle offers and create a balance that suits your needs.

Continuously Iterate and Improve:
The journey of optimizing your time management and productivity is an ongoing process. Regularly review and assess your strategies to identify areas for improvement. Experiment with new techniques and tools to find what works best for you. Stay open to change and adapt your approach as needed to maximize your efficiency and effectiveness.

By applying the principles shared in "The 4-Hour Work Week," you can transform the way you manage your time and accomplish tasks as a digital nomad. Remember that these strategies are not one-size-fits-all, so experiment and find what works best for your unique circumstances. Through continuous refinement and a focus on high-impact activities, you can create a fulfilling and successful digital nomad lifestyle.

CHAPTER 13: PURSUING YOUR PASSION: FINDING WORK YOU LOVE

In this chapter, we will explore the significance of aligning your work with your passions and interests as a digital nomad. When you find work that ignites your enthusiasm and aligns with your values, it transforms your entire nomadic journey. Let's discuss practical guidance on discovering and pursuing your true passions.

Reflect on Your Interests and Values:
Start by taking the time to reflect on your interests, values, and what brings you joy. What activities make you lose track of time? What topics or causes ignite your curiosity? Consider your core values and how they align with potential career paths. This self-reflection will help you identify areas of passion that you can incorporate into your work as a digital nomad.

Explore Different Industries and Opportunities:
Once you have a general idea of your passions, explore different industries and opportunities that resonate with those interests. Conduct research, read books, attend webinars, and engage with online communities related to your areas of curiosity. By immersing yourself in these spaces, you can gain insights into potential career paths that align with your passions.

Seek Inspiration from Others:
Look for inspiring individuals who have successfully combined their passions with their work as digital nomads. Follow their journeys through blogs, podcasts, and social media platforms. Study their experiences, learn from their successes and challenges, and draw inspiration from their stories. This can provide valuable insights and motivate you to pursue your own path.

Experiment and Take Action:
Don't be afraid to experiment and try different things. Start small by taking on passion projects or side gigs related to your interests. This allows you to test the waters and gain practical experience. As a digital nomad, you have the freedom to explore various opportunities and iterate until you find the right fit. Taking action is key to discovering your true passions.

Network and Collaborate:
Connect with like-minded individuals who share your passions. Attend conferences, join online communities, and participate in industry events. Engage in conversations, share your ideas, and collaborate with others who can support and inspire you. Networking opens doors to new opportunities and provides valuable connections within your chosen field.

Embrace Continuous Learning:
To pursue your passions effectively, commit to lifelong learning. Stay updated with industry trends, technologies, and skills relevant to your interests. Take online courses, attend workshops, and read books that deepen your knowledge and expertise. Continuous learning enhances your credibility and keeps you engaged with your passion-driven work.

Combine Passions and Skills:
Look for ways to merge your passions with your existing skills or expertise. Identify the unique value you can bring to the table by combining different areas of interest. For example, if you have a passion for writing and a background in marketing, you could explore content creation or digital marketing roles that allow you to express your creativity while leveraging your skills.

Test the Viability of Your Passion-Driven Work:
While pursuing your passions is important, it's essential to assess the market viability of your chosen path. Evaluate if there is a demand for your passion-driven work and explore potential niches within your chosen field. Conduct market research,

analyze competition, and identify how you can offer unique value to your target audience.

Embrace the Journey:
Finding work you love is a continuous journey of self-discovery and growth. Embrace the ups and downs, knowing that it takes time to align your passions with your work. Stay resilient, adapt to new opportunities, and be open to evolving your path as you gain more insights and experiences.

Remember, finding work you love as a digital nomad is a dynamic process. It requires self-reflection, exploration, and experimentation. By aligning your passions with your work, you can experience greater fulfillment, purpose, and motivation in your nomadic lifestyle. Take the first step today towards discovering and pursuing your true passions as a digital nomad.

CHAPTER 14: THE 80/20 PRINCIPLE: MAXIMIZING PRODUCTIVITY

In this chapter, we will explore the concept of the 80/20 principle and how it can significantly enhance your productivity as a digital nomad. The 80/20 principle, also known as the Pareto Principle, states that roughly 80% of your results come from 20% of your efforts. By understanding and applying this principle to your work and life, you can prioritize your tasks effectively, focus on what truly matters, and achieve remarkable outcomes. Let's delve into practical examples of identifying and focusing on the most impactful tasks.

Identify Your Key Objectives:
Begin by identifying your key objectives or goals. What are the most important outcomes you want to achieve? Whether it's completing a project, launching a product, or growing your client base, clearly define your top priorities. By having a clear understanding of your objectives, you can align your efforts accordingly.

Analyze Task Importance and Impact:
Take a closer look at your to-do list and assess the importance and impact of each task. Ask yourself: Which tasks contribute the most to achieving my key objectives? Which tasks have the highest potential for driving significant results? By evaluating the importance and impact of each task, you can determine the 20% that will generate 80% of your desired outcomes.

Delegate or Eliminate Non-Essential Tasks:
Identify tasks that do not align with your key objectives or have a minimal impact on your desired outcomes. Delegate these tasks to others if possible, or eliminate them altogether. Delegating non-essential tasks frees up your time and energy to focus on the critical 20% that drives the majority of your results.

Leverage the Power of Outsourcing:
As a digital nomad, you have access to a global talent pool. Consider outsourcing tasks that are not within your core competencies or require a significant amount of time. Platforms like Upwork, Fiverr, and Freelancer provide access to a wide range of freelancers who can assist with various tasks, such as graphic design, content writing, or administrative work. By outsourcing non-essential tasks, you can concentrate on activities that leverage your unique skills and expertise.

Prioritize High-Impact Tasks:
Once you have identified the tasks that contribute the most to your desired outcomes, prioritize them. Focus on completing these high-impact tasks first. This ensures that you allocate your time and energy to the activities that generate the greatest results. By tackling the most impactful tasks early on, you set yourself up for productivity and success.

Use Time Blocking:
Time blocking is a valuable technique that helps you allocate specific time slots for different tasks or activities. Schedule dedicated blocks of time for your high-impact tasks and guard those time blocks against distractions. During these focused periods, eliminate interruptions, silence notifications, and create an environment conducive to deep work. Time blocking enhances your productivity by providing structure and dedicated time for important tasks.

Embrace the Power of Single-Tasking:
Multitasking can be counterproductive and diminish your focus and efficiency. Instead, embrace the power of single-tasking. Dedicate your attention to one task at a time, giving it your full focus and concentration. By avoiding the temptation to switch between multiple tasks, you can maintain a higher level of productivity and produce higher-quality work.

Leverage Productivity Tools and Apps:

There are numerous productivity tools and apps available to help you streamline your workflow and maximize efficiency. Explore applications like Trello, Asana, or Todoist for task management and project collaboration. Utilize time-tracking apps like Toggl or RescueTime to monitor and optimize your time usage. Experiment with different tools and find the ones that best suit your needs and preferences.

Remember, the key to leveraging the 80/20 principle is not simply about being busy or working harder. It's about working smarter and focusing your efforts on the tasks that yield the greatest impact. By identifying and prioritizing the most significant activities, outsourcing non-essential tasks, and embracing productivity-enhancing techniques, you can optimize your workflow and achieve exceptional results as a digital nomad.

CHAPTER 15: AUTOMATION AND DELEGATION: WORKING SMARTER, NOT HARDER

In today's fast-paced world, the ability to work smarter, not harder, is crucial for digital nomads seeking to optimize their productivity and achieve a healthy work-life balance. This chapter explores the benefits of automation and delegation and provides practical tips for identifying tasks to automate or delegate, as well as finding reliable support. By leveraging these strategies, you can free up valuable time and energy to focus on activities that truly matter.

Understanding the Benefits of Automation:
Automation involves utilizing technology and systems to streamline repetitive or time-consuming tasks. By automating certain processes, you can reduce manual effort, minimize errors, and increase efficiency. Consider the following areas where automation can be particularly beneficial:

a. Email Management: Use email filters, canned responses, and email scheduling tools to manage your inbox more effectively. Set up rules to automatically sort and prioritize incoming emails, reducing the time spent on manual organization.

b. Social Media Posting: Utilize social media management tools like Hootsuite or Buffer to schedule and automate your social media posts across multiple platforms. This allows you to maintain a consistent online presence without spending excessive time on daily postings.

c. Financial Tracking: Take advantage of accounting software like QuickBooks or FreshBooks to automate financial tracking, invoicing, and expense management. These tools can streamline your financial processes and provide a clear overview of your income and expenses.

d. Task Management: Implement task management tools such as Todoist or Asana to create automated workflows, assign tasks, and track progress. These platforms enable you to streamline collaboration and stay organized.

Identifying Tasks for Automation:
Start by assessing your daily workflow and identifying tasks that are repetitive, time-consuming, or can be easily systematized. Consider the following areas where automation can significantly enhance your productivity:

a. Data Entry and Reporting: Look for opportunities to automate data entry and reporting processes. For instance, use tools like Zapier or Integromat to integrate different software applications and automate data transfer between them.

b. Social Media Engagement: While automation can be useful for scheduling posts, it's important to balance it with genuine engagement. Instead of automating interactions, prioritize real-time engagement with your audience to build authentic connections.

c. Content Creation: Leverage content creation tools like Grammarly or Hemingway Editor to automate grammar and style checks, saving time on editing and proofreading. Additionally, consider using AI-powered writing tools to generate content outlines or drafts.

d. Customer Support: Implement chatbot systems or AI-powered customer support tools to automate routine inquiries and provide immediate responses. However, ensure that there is always a human touch available for complex or personalized customer interactions.

Harnessing the Power of Delegation:
Delegation is a key skill for digital nomads seeking to work smarter and focus on their core strengths. Here are practical tips for identifying tasks to delegate and finding reliable support:

a. Task Evaluation: Assess your task list and determine which tasks can be delegated to others. Identify activities that are outside your expertise or consume excessive time, such as administrative work, graphic design, or content creation.

b. Outsourcing Platforms: Explore online outsourcing platforms like Upwork, Freelancer, or Fiverr to find talented freelancers or virtual assistants who can assist with specific tasks. Clearly define the scope of work and expectations to ensure a smooth working relationship.

c. Building a Virtual Team: Consider assembling a virtual team of specialists to support your business. This may include web developers, graphic designers, copywriters, or social media managers. Collaborating with a dedicated team can help you scale your business and leverage diverse expertise.

d. Communication and Collaboration: Establish effective communication channels with your team, such as project management tools or video conferencing platforms. Regularly communicate expectations, provide feedback, and ensure that everyone is aligned with the goals and timelines.

Remember, automation and delegation are not about relinquishing control, but rather about optimizing your time and energy. By automating repetitive tasks and delegating non-core activities, you can focus on high value work, personal growth, and nurturing relationships. Working smarter, not harder, is the key to achieving sustainable success and enjoying the freedom that the digital nomad lifestyle offers.

CHAPTER 16: CREATING EFFECTIVE TO-DO AND NOT-TO-DO LISTS

Effective time management is a critical skill for digital nomads seeking to maximize their productivity and maintain a healthy work-life balance. In this chapter, we will explore the importance of prioritization and time management by creating efficient to-do and not-to-do lists. These lists will help you stay focused on essential tasks while eliminating non-essential ones, ensuring that your time and energy are dedicated to what truly matters.

The Power of Prioritization:
Prioritization is the key to effective time management. It allows you to identify and focus on tasks that have the most significant impact on your goals and overall productivity. Here are practical techniques to help you prioritize effectively:

a. Eisenhower Matrix: The Eisenhower Matrix is a powerful tool for prioritization. Divide your tasks into four categories: urgent and important, important but not urgent, urgent but not important, and neither urgent nor important. Focus your efforts on tasks that fall into the urgent and important quadrant.

b. ABC Method: Assign priorities to your tasks using the ABC method. Label tasks as A, B, or C, with A being the most important and C being the least. Prioritize and tackle your A tasks before moving on to B and C tasks.

c. Time Blocking: Allocate specific time blocks for different tasks or categories of work. Dedicate focused periods to high-priority tasks, minimizing distractions during those intervals. This technique helps you maintain a structured schedule and prioritize tasks accordingly.

Creating an Effective To-Do List:
A well-structured to-do list is an invaluable tool for organizing

your day and keeping track of your tasks. Follow these practical techniques to create an efficient to-do list:

a. Clear and Specific Tasks: Ensure that each task on your list is clear and specific. Avoid vague descriptions that may lead to confusion or procrastination. Instead, break down larger tasks into smaller actionable steps.

b. Order of Priority: Arrange your tasks in order of priority, based on the techniques mentioned earlier. Start with the most important tasks and work your way down the list. By tackling high-priority tasks first, you maintain focus and accomplish critical work early in the day.

c. Realistic Expectations: Be realistic when setting expectations for your to-do list. Consider the time and resources required for each task, and avoid overloading your schedule. By setting achievable goals, you reduce stress and increase the likelihood of completing tasks successfully.

d. Deadlines and Reminders: Attach deadlines or reminders to your tasks, especially for time-sensitive assignments. Use digital tools like calendars or task management apps to stay on top of deadlines and receive notifications that keep you accountable.

The Power of Not-to-Do Lists:
Just as important as knowing what to prioritize is understanding what to eliminate or minimize. Not-to-do lists are an effective way to identify non-essential tasks or distractions that hinder your productivity. Here are practical techniques for creating a not-to-do list:

a. Identify Time Wasters: Reflect on your daily routines and identify activities that waste your time or distract you from your goals. This may include excessive social media usage, unproductive meetings, or certain non-essential tasks that can be delegated or eliminated.

b. Delegate or Outsource: Determine tasks that can be delegated to others or outsourced. Focus on your core strengths and responsibilities, and consider if there are any activities that can be passed on to capable team members or freelancers.

c. Set Boundaries: Establish clear boundaries to protect your time and energy. Learn to say no to non-essential commitments or requests that do not align with your priorities or values. Setting boundaries helps you maintain focus on what truly matters.

d. Limit Distractions: Identify common distractions in your work environment and find strategies to minimize their impact. This may include turning off notifications, designating specific times for checking emails or messages, or using website blockers to avoid time-consuming websites during work hours.

By implementing these techniques for creating effective to-do and not-to-do lists, you can enhance your productivity, maintain focus on essential tasks, and eliminate unnecessary time-wasting activities. Remember, effective time management is a continuous process of self-reflection and adjustment. Regularly review and update your lists to adapt to changing priorities and optimize your digital nomad lifestyle.

CHAPTER 17: EVALUATING YOUR NOMADIC LIFESTYLE

As a digital nomad, it is crucial to periodically assess your nomadic lifestyle to ensure it aligns with your goals, values, and long-term sustainability. Evaluating your experiences allows you to make informed decisions, make necessary adjustments, and find fulfillment in your journey. In this chapter, we will guide you through practical reflection exercises and considerations for evaluating your nomadic lifestyle.

Clarify Your Goals:
Begin by revisiting your goals and aspirations as a digital nomad. Reflect on why you chose this lifestyle and what you initially hoped to achieve. Take the time to reassess and realign your goals if needed. Consider the following questions:

What are your short-term and long-term goals as a digital nomad?
Have your goals evolved or changed since you started your nomadic journey?
Do you feel a sense of fulfillment and purpose in your current lifestyle?
By gaining clarity on your goals, you can evaluate whether your nomadic lifestyle is helping you move closer to them.

Assess Work-Life Balance:
One of the primary benefits of the digital nomad lifestyle is the ability to have more control over your work-life balance. Evaluate how well you are maintaining this balance and whether adjustments are necessary. Consider the following points:

Are you dedicating enough time to self-care, hobbies, and personal growth?
Do you feel overwhelmed or burnt out from work-related responsibilities?

Are you able to disconnect from work and enjoy your travel experiences?

Take practical steps to address any imbalances and ensure that your nomadic lifestyle supports your overall well-being.

Financial Sustainability:

Evaluate the financial sustainability of your nomadic lifestyle. Assess your income streams, expenses, and financial goals. Consider the following aspects:

Are your current income sources sufficient to support your desired lifestyle?

Have you built a solid financial foundation for emergencies and unexpected expenses?

Are there opportunities to diversify or increase your income streams?

It is important to have a clear understanding of your financial situation to make informed decisions and ensure long-term sustainability as a digital nomad.

Social Connections:

Assess the quality of your social connections and support networks. Nomadic living can sometimes lead to a transient lifestyle, making it important to cultivate meaningful relationships. Reflect on the following:

Do you have a supportive community of fellow digital nomads or like-minded individuals?

Are you able to establish and maintain relationships with locals in the places you visit?

Do you feel connected and supported in both your online and offline communities?

Actively seek opportunities to foster connections and create a sense of belonging wherever you go.

Environmental Impact:

Consider the environmental impact of your nomadic lifestyle. Evaluate your practices and habits to ensure you are minimizing your ecological footprint. Reflect on the following:

Are you mindful of your consumption and waste management while traveling?
Do you make sustainable choices when it comes to transportation, accommodation, and daily activities?
Are there ways you can further reduce your impact on the environment?
Strive to be an environmentally conscious digital nomad and contribute positively to the places you visit.

Personal Growth and Learning:
Assess the extent to which your nomadic lifestyle has contributed to your personal growth and learning. Reflect on the following:

Have you acquired new skills or knowledge through your experiences as a digital nomad?
Are you actively seeking personal and professional development opportunities?
Do you feel a sense of continuous learning and growth in your current lifestyle?
Embrace opportunities for growth and invest in your personal and professional development.

Revisiting Your Values:
Revisit your core values and evaluate whether your nomadic lifestyle aligns with them. Reflect on the following:

Are you living in alignment with your values and principles?
Have your values evolved or changed since adopting the nomadic lifestyle?
Are there any aspects of your lifestyle that feel incongruent with your values?
Aligning your actions with your values fosters a sense of authenticity and fulfillment.

By engaging in this evaluation process, you will gain a deeper understanding of your nomadic lifestyle and its impact on various aspects of your life. Use this reflection as a guide for making intentional decisions and adjustments along your digital nomad journey. Remember that your nomadic lifestyle should evolve with you, reflecting your goals, values, and aspirations, ultimately leading to a fulfilling and sustainable way of living.

CHAPTER 18: BUILDING SELF-BELIEF AND OVERCOMING DOUBTS

Self-belief is the cornerstone of success as a digital nomad. It empowers us to overcome challenges, take risks, and pursue our dreams with confidence. In this chapter, we will explore the importance of self-belief in achieving success as a digital nomad and provide practical strategies for building confidence and overcoming self-doubt.

Reflect on Your Strengths:
Begin by reflecting on your unique strengths and capabilities. Consider the following points:

What are your core skills and areas of expertise?
What past experiences have demonstrated your competence and resourcefulness?
How have you overcome challenges in the past?
By acknowledging your strengths, you build a foundation of self-belief and recognize the value you bring to your digital nomad journey.

Cultivate a Growth Mindset:
Embracing a growth mindset is crucial for building self-belief. Understand that skills and abilities can be developed through effort and learning. Consider the following actions:

Embrace challenges as opportunities for growth and learning.
View setbacks as temporary and treat them as learning experiences.
Emphasize the process of improvement rather than focusing solely on outcomes.
By adopting a growth mindset, you foster resilience and believe in your capacity to continually evolve as a digital nomad.

Seek Positive Feedback:

Actively seek out and appreciate positive feedback from clients, colleagues, and mentors. Consider the following steps:

Request feedback from clients or customers on your work or services.
Connect with other digital nomads or professionals in your field for constructive feedback.
Keep a record of positive testimonials or reviews to remind yourself of your competence.
Positive feedback serves as validation and reinforces your self-belief, reminding you of the value you provide.

Set Realistic Goals:
Setting realistic and achievable goals is essential for building self-belief. Consider the following strategies:

Break down larger goals into smaller, manageable milestones.
Set specific and measurable objectives that align with your vision.
Celebrate and acknowledge progress as you reach each milestone.
By achieving smaller goals along the way, you strengthen your belief in your ability to accomplish more significant objectives.

Embrace Continuous Learning:
Commit to lifelong learning and skill development. Consider the following approaches:

Stay updated on industry trends and advancements in your field.
Attend workshops, webinars, or conferences related to your areas of interest.
Invest time in reading books, listening to podcasts, or taking online courses.
Continuous learning not only enhances your expertise but also boosts your confidence and self-belief.

Practice Visualization and Affirmations:
Visualization and positive affirmations can be powerful tools for building self-belief. Consider the following practices:

Visualize yourself successfully overcoming challenges and

achieving your goals.
Create affirmations that reinforce your capabilities and potential. Repeat these affirmations daily and visualize your success during meditation or quiet reflection.
By consistently practicing visualization and affirmations, you rewire your mind for success and strengthen your self-belief.

Surround Yourself with Supportive Communities:
Surrounding yourself with supportive communities can significantly impact your self-belief. Consider the following actions:

Join digital nomad groups or online communities where you can connect with like-minded individuals.
Attend meetups or events where you can network with fellow digital nomads.
Seek out mentors or coaches who can provide guidance and support.
Being part of supportive communities fosters a sense of belonging, encouragement, and shared experiences, reinforcing your self-belief.

Embrace Failure as Growth:
Embrace failure as an opportunity for growth rather than a reflection of your worth. Consider the following approaches:

Reframe failures as learning experiences and opportunities for growth.
Analyze what went wrong and extract lessons from each setback.
View failure as a necessary and normal part of the learning process.
By reframing your perception of failure, you can bounce back stronger, armed with valuable insights and increased self-belief.

Take Action Despite Fear:
Finally, one of the most effective ways to build self-belief is by taking action, even in the face of fear and uncertainty. Consider the following steps:

Identify one area where self-doubt is holding you back.
Break down the desired action into smaller, manageable steps.
Take the first step, regardless of any fear or doubts you may have. Each action you take, no matter how small, reinforces your belief in your ability to navigate the challenges of the digital nomad lifestyle.

Building self-belief is a fundamental pillar of success as a digital nomad. By recognizing your achievements, surrounding yourself with supportive people, challenging limiting beliefs, embracing continuous learning, celebrating small wins, embracing failure, and taking action despite fear, you can cultivate a strong sense of self-belief. Remember that self-belief is not an overnight achievement but a lifelong journey of personal growth and development. Through consistent effort and practice, you can overcome doubts and unlock your true potential as a confident and successful digital nomad.

CHAPTER 19: FOLLOWING YOUR PASSION: TAKING BOLD ACTION

Passion is a powerful force that drives us to pursue our dreams and find fulfillment in our work and lives. In this chapter, we will explore the importance of following your passion and provide practical steps for taking bold action towards your passions. Let's dive into how you can ignite your passion and make significant changes in your life.

Identify Your Passions:
Start by reflecting on your interests, values, and what truly excites you. Consider the following points:

What activities or subjects bring you joy and fulfillment?
What issues or causes do you feel deeply passionate about?
What skills or talents do you possess that you want to explore further?
Take the time to explore and identify your passions. This self-awareness will serve as a compass for the actions you'll take.

Define Your Vision:
Once you have identified your passions, it's essential to envision what your ideal future looks like. Consider the following steps:

Imagine yourself living a life aligned with your passions.
Visualize the impact you want to make in the world.
Set specific goals that reflect your passion-driven vision.
Defining your vision provides clarity and direction, fueling your motivation to take bold action.

Break Down Your Goals:
To turn your passion into a reality, break down your goals into actionable steps. Consider the following strategies:

Divide your larger goals into smaller, achievable milestones.

Outline the specific tasks and actions required to reach each milestone.
Set deadlines and create a timeline for accomplishing each step.
Breaking down your goals into manageable chunks makes them less daunting and increases your likelihood of success.

Overcome Fear and Resistance:
Taking bold action requires overcoming fear and resistance. Consider the following approaches:

Recognize that fear is a normal part of the journey and embrace it as an opportunity for growth.
Challenge limiting beliefs and replace them with empowering thoughts.
Surround yourself with supportive individuals who believe in your passion and can offer guidance.
By acknowledging and confronting your fears, you can move forward with courage and confidence.

Take the First Step:
The first step is often the hardest, but it's crucial in initiating change. Consider the following actions:

Identify the smallest action you can take right now towards your passion.
Make a commitment to take that step, no matter how small it may seem.
Celebrate your courage and progress once you've taken that initial action.
Taking the first step creates momentum and propels you further along the path of following your passion.

Embrace Continuous Learning:
To pursue your passion effectively, commit to continuous learning and skill development. Consider the following strategies:

Seek out resources, courses, or mentors related to your passion.
Stay up-to-date with industry trends and advancements in your

field.
Network with like-minded individuals and learn from their experiences.
Embracing continuous learning ensures that you're equipped with the knowledge and skills needed to excel in your passion pursuit.

Embody Perseverance:
Following your passion requires perseverance and resilience in the face of challenges. Consider the following practices:

View obstacles as opportunities for growth and learning.
Stay committed to your passion, even when the going gets tough.
Seek support from mentors, peers, or communities that can provide encouragement and guidance.
Embodying perseverance allows you to overcome setbacks and stay dedicated to your passion-driven journey.

Iterate and Adapt:
As you progress on your passion-driven path, be open to iterating and adapting your approach. Consider the following mindset:

Reflect on your experiences and adjust your strategies as needed.
Embrace flexibility and be willing to explore new avenues within your passion.
Emphasize the journey as much as the destination, allowing yourself to evolve and grow along the way.
Iteration and adaptation ensure that your actions align with your evolving passion and vision.

Taking bold action towards your passion is a transformative and fulfilling endeavor. By identifying your passions, defining your vision, breaking down your goals, overcoming fear and resistance, taking the first step, embracing continuous learning, embodying perseverance, and iterating and adapting along the way, you can navigate the path of following your passion with confidence and purpose. Remember, this journey is yours to embrace and savor as you make significant changes in your life.

CHAPTER 20: MAKING A DIFFERENCE: HELPING OTHERS AND LEAVING A LEGACY

Throughout your journey of escaping the matrix and embracing the digital nomad lifestyle, it's essential to recognize the importance of contributing to the world and making a positive impact. In this final chapter, we will explore how you can use your skills and resources as a digital nomad to help others and leave a meaningful legacy. Let's dive into the ways you can make a difference and create a lasting positive influence.

Identify Your Impact Areas:
Start by reflecting on the causes and issues that resonate with you. Consider the following steps:

Identify the areas where you can make a meaningful impact based on your skills, interests, and values.

Research local and global organizations or initiatives that align with your chosen impact areas.

Evaluate how your digital nomad lifestyle can be leveraged to address specific challenges and contribute to positive change.

By identifying your impact areas, you can focus your efforts on creating a difference where it matters most to you.

Volunteer Your Skills:
As a digital nomad, you possess a valuable set of skills that can benefit organizations and communities in need. Consider the following approaches:

Seek out volunteering opportunities with organizations that align with your impact areas.

Offer your expertise in areas such as web design, social media management, content creation, or digital marketing.

Consider pro bono work for nonprofit organizations or grassroots initiatives that could benefit from your skills.

Volunteering your skills allows you to contribute to meaningful projects while honing your abilities and expanding your network.

Share Knowledge and Mentorship:
Another impactful way to make a difference is by sharing your knowledge and providing mentorship to others. Consider the following strategies:

Offer workshops, webinars, or online courses related to your expertise.
Create educational content or tutorials that can benefit aspiring digital nomads or entrepreneurs.
Seek mentorship opportunities where you can guide and support individuals who share your passions.
Sharing knowledge and mentorship empowers others to pursue their dreams and fosters a sense of community and collaboration.

Support Local Economies:
As a digital nomad, you have the opportunity to contribute to local economies and communities wherever you go. Consider the following actions:

Choose local businesses, cafes, and services over multinational chains whenever possible.
Engage with local artisans and craftsmen, supporting their work and preserving cultural heritage.
Explore opportunities to collaborate with local entrepreneurs and freelancers, fostering mutual growth.
By supporting local economies, you not only contribute directly to the well-being of communities but also promote sustainable and responsible tourism.

Environmental Stewardship:
Recognize the impact of your actions on the environment and embrace practices that minimize your ecological footprint. Consider the following steps:

Adopt eco-friendly habits, such as reducing single-use

plastic, conserving energy, and practicing responsible waste management.
Engage in initiatives that promote environmental conservation and sustainability.
Educate others about the importance of environmental stewardship and inspire them to take action.
By being conscious of your environmental impact and advocating for sustainable practices, you contribute to the well-being of the planet and future generations.

Philanthropic Initiatives:
Consider supporting philanthropic initiatives or starting your own projects that address social or environmental challenges. Consider the following actions:

Donate a portion of your income to causes you care about.
Launch crowdfunding campaigns to fund projects that align with your impact areas.
Collaborate with other digital nomads or organizations to create collective initiatives that have a greater impact.
Engaging in philanthropic initiatives allows you to make a direct and tangible difference in the lives of others.

Document and Share Inspiring Stories:
Finally, leverage your skills as a digital nomad to document and share inspiring stories of individuals or communities making a difference. Consider the following approaches:

Create compelling multimedia content that highlights impactful initiatives and raises awareness.
Interview changemakers and share their stories through blog posts, podcasts, or videos.
Use storytelling as a tool to inspire others to take action and contribute to positive change.
By amplifying the voices of those creating a difference, you inspire and mobilize others to join the movement.

Remember, making a difference is not limited to grand gestures but rather encompasses the cumulative impact of consistent actions, big and small. As a digital nomad, you have the unique opportunity to navigate the world while leaving a positive footprint. By identifying your impact areas, volunteering your skills, sharing knowledge, supporting local economies, practicing environmental stewardship, engaging in philanthropy, and documenting inspiring stories, you can contribute to a better world and leave a lasting legacy.

This book has provided you with practical guidance and insights on how to escape the matrix and embrace the freedom of the digital nomad lifestyle. By taking action, following your passions, and making a positive impact, you have the power to live life on your own terms, create a meaningful existence, and inspire others to do the same. Embrace the journey, be bold, and shape your own destiny. The world awaits your unique contributions.

CONCLUSION

In this journey of escaping the matrix and embracing the digital nomad lifestyle, you have embarked on a path of self-discovery, freedom, and limitless possibilities. Throughout this book, we have explored numerous practical strategies, shared inspiring stories, and provided guidance to help you navigate this transformative journey. Now, as we conclude this book, let's recap the key principles and lessons we have discussed and ignite the fire within you to embrace the freedom of the digital nomad lifestyle and live life on your own terms.

Taking Action: Becoming the Chooser, Not the Chosen:
We have emphasized the importance of taking action and developing a proactive mindset. It's not enough to merely indulge in thoughts and ideas. By stepping out of your comfort zone and actively choosing your path, you become the driver of your own life. Remember, action is the catalyst for change.

Embracing Remote Work and Being Your Own Boss:
We explored the benefits of remote work, allowing you to escape the constraints of traditional office jobs. We shared practical tips for finding remote work opportunities and establishing yourself as a freelancer or entrepreneur. Embrace the flexibility and autonomy that remote work provides, enabling you to design your work-life balance.

Making the Most of Your Resources:
Travel is a core aspect of the digital nomad lifestyle. We discussed the financial advantages of living and working in lower-cost locations and provided practical examples of budgeting and managing expenses. Optimize your resources and make conscious choices to ensure that every travel experience contributes to your personal growth and fulfillment.

Building Passive Income Streams:
Generating passive income is key to sustaining your digital nomad lifestyle. We explored various avenues such as writing a book, creating online products, and investing in rental properties. By diversifying your income sources and setting up systems that generate income while you focus on your passions, you can create a foundation for long-term financial independence.

Breaking Free from News Consumption:
Excessive news consumption can hinder personal growth and well-being. We provided practical strategies for reducing news intake and focusing on positive and constructive information. Remember to prioritize your mental and emotional well-being by curating a media diet that nourishes your mind and fosters inspiration.

Balancing Online and Offline Life:
In an increasingly digital world, we highlighted the importance of maintaining real-world connections and experiences. We suggested practical ways to limit social media usage and prioritize face-to-face interactions. Nurture authentic relationships, immerse yourself in local cultures, and seek meaningful connections that enrich your nomadic journey.

Embracing Minimalism: Living with Less:
We discussed the benefits of living a simple and minimalist lifestyle. Practical tips for decluttering, organizing, and finding happiness in non-materialistic pursuits were shared. Embrace minimalism not only in your physical possessions but also in your mindset, freeing yourself from the burden of excess and focusing on what truly matters.

Leading instead of Following: Trailblazing Your Path:
Embrace your innate leadership qualities and forge your own path. We explored the advantages of being a leader rather than a follower in personal and professional life. Take initiative, embrace calculated risks, and let your unique voice and vision guide you

towards success and fulfillment.

Overcoming External Limitations: Dealing with Family and Friends:
Breaking free from societal expectations and well-meaning but limiting influences can be challenging. We offered practical advice on how to communicate with loved ones and gain their support for your chosen path. Remember, your journey is unique, and by nurturing open and honest relationships, you can seek understanding and build a strong support system.

Embracing Life's Mystery: Finding Meaning in the Unknown:
Life is full of uncertainties and unknowns. We discussed the existential aspect of life and encouraged you to find joy in the journey. Embrace the mysteries, explore new horizons, and seek personal growth and fulfillment through the experiences and challenges that come your way.

Preparing for the Digital Nomad Lifestyle:
Practical advice on financial, emotional, and logistical preparation was shared. We discussed potential challenges and how to overcome them. By being prepared and adaptable, you can navigate the nomadic lifestyle with confidence and resilience.

The Essence of the 4-Hour Work Week:
We explained the key principles of Tim Ferriss' book and how they can be applied to the digital nomad lifestyle. Practical examples of time management and productivity strategies were provided. Optimize your work hours, focus on high-impact tasks, and create a life where work serves your desired lifestyle, rather than the other way around.

Pursuing Your Passion: Finding Work You Love:
Aligning your work with your passions and interests is crucial for a fulfilling nomadic lifestyle. We discussed the importance of discovering and pursuing your true passions. Embrace the freedom to choose work that brings you joy and purpose, and cultivate a career that energizes and motivates you each day.

The 80/20 Principle: Maximizing Productivity:
We explained the concept of the 80/20 principle and how it can be applied to work and life. Practical examples of identifying and focusing on the most impactful tasks were shared. By prioritizing your efforts and focusing on what truly matters, you can maximize your productivity and achieve meaningful results.

Automation and Delegation: Working Smarter, Not Harder:
We discussed the benefits of automating and delegating tasks to free up time and energy. Practical tips for identifying tasks to automate or delegate and finding reliable support were offered. By leveraging technology and delegating non-essential tasks, you can create space for creativity, growth, and a balanced lifestyle.

Creating Effective To-Do and Not-to-Do Lists:
Highlighting the importance of prioritization and time management, we provided practical techniques for creating efficient to-do lists and eliminating non-essential tasks. By focusing on what truly matters and consciously removing distractions, you can optimize your time and energy to achieve your goals.

Evaluating Your Nomadic Lifestyle:
We guided you in assessing your experiences as a digital nomad and determining if it's the right fit for you. Practical reflection exercises and considerations for long-term sustainability were provided. Regular evaluation helps you align your lifestyle with your evolving values and aspirations, ensuring that your nomadic journey remains fulfilling and meaningful.

Building Self-Belief and Overcoming Doubts:
We discussed the importance of self-belief in achieving success as a digital nomad. Practical strategies for building confidence and overcoming self-doubt were shared. Cultivate self-compassion, embrace personal growth, and celebrate your accomplishments along the way.

Following Your Passion: Taking Bold Action:
Encouragement to pursue your passions boldly and fearlessly was given. Practical steps for taking action and making significant changes in your life were provided. Embrace the courage within you, step outside your comfort zone, and let your passions guide you towards a life of purpose and fulfillment.

Making a Difference: Helping Others and Leaving a Legacy:
In this final chapter, we discussed the importance of contributing to the world and making a positive impact. Practical examples of how digital nomads can use their skills and resources to help others were shared. By leveraging your unique position as a digital nomad, you have the power to leave a lasting legacy and create positive change in the lives of others.

As we conclude this book, I hope you feel inspired and empowered to embrace the freedom of the digital nomad lifestyle. Remember, the journey may have its challenges, but with determination, adaptability, and a passion for growth, you can create a life on your own terms. Embrace the unknown, seize opportunities, and let the world become your playground. The digital nomad lifestyle is not just a means of escape; it is a doorway to self-discovery, personal freedom, and a life filled with unforgettable experiences. So, take the leap, spread your wings, and embark on this extraordinary adventure. The power to escape the matrix and live life on your own terms is within your reach. Embrace the freedom, embrace the possibilities, and embrace a life that is uniquely yours.